young Trailblazers

The Book of
Black Heroes and Groundbreakers

Young Trailblazers

The Book of Black Heroes and Groundbreakers

By M.J. Fievre

Illustrations by Kim Balacuit

CORAL GABLES

Cover, illustration, and layout design: Kim Balacuit
Images used under license from Adobe Stock

For permission requests, please contact the publisher at:
Mango Publishing Group
2850 S Douglas Road, 4th Floor
Coral Gables, FL 33134 USA
info@mango.bz

For special orders, quantity sales, course adoptions and corporate
sales, please email the publisher at sales@mango.bz. For trade
and wholesale sales, please contact Ingram Publisher Services at
customer.service@ingramcontent.com or +1.800.509.4887.

Young Trailblazers: The Book of Black Heroes and Groundbreakers

Library of Congress Cataloging-in-Publication number: 2021946712
ISBN: (print) 978-1-64250-782-9 (ebook) 978-1-64250-783-6
BISAC category code JNF025190, JUVENILE NONFICTION / History /
United States / Colonial & Revolutionary Periods

Printed in the United States of America

Contents

 Introduction

Heroes and Groundbreakers

America inherited the strength, courage, wisdom, love, and dignity of our Black heroes and overcomers. We stand on their shoulders—these creators, innovators, and agents of change—and, because of their tremendous struggle, we are strong and can conquer whatever challenges this world hands us.

Let us never forget those who broke the unjust rules society used (and sometimes still uses) to limit our progress, those who fought hard to get us to this moment, those who gave light so others could find the way through dark times.

Because of them, all of us can hope to walk in the freedom they fought for, and continue to fight for, on our behalf.

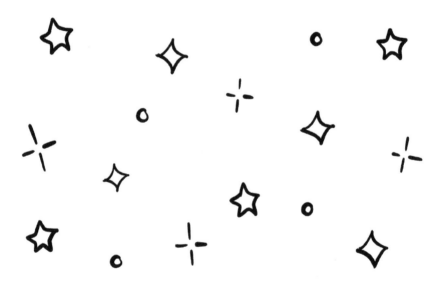

Alice Allison Dunnigan

Alice **Allison Dunnigan** was a journalist, civil rights activist, and author. She was born in 1906 near Russellville, Kentucky. Her father was a sharecropper, and her mother took in laundry to make money. Despite this, her family was not as poor as many of the families surrounding them. They owned their own home. Alice began attending school one day a week when she was four years old and was able to read before she entered the first grade. When she was just thirteen years old, she began writing for a local paper, the *Owensboro Enterprise*. After she graduated from high school, Alice took a teaching certification course at the Kentucky Normal and Industrial Institute. She taught Kentucky history in the Todd County school system, but Alice noticed that none of the history books included the contributions of Black people, so she included supplemental sheets that she wrote for her students with information about the contributions of Black people in Kentucky. In 1942, during **World War II**, she answered a call from the federal government for people to take up government jobs and move to Washington, DC. She left Kentucky for a better-paying government job in 1942. Alice worked at a government job from 1942 to 1946 and took night courses at **Howard University**.

Words You Should Know

» A sharecropper is someone who rents a parcel of land from a farmer and pays their rent with a portion of their crops. After the Civil War, many former slaves became sharecroppers on their former owners' plantations.

In 1946, the *Chicago Defender*, a **Black-owned newspaper**, offered her a position as its Washington correspondent, but she received less pay than her coworkers because she was new to journalism. Alice had to fight hard to get press credentials to cover the House of Representatives and the Senate. Her first application was denied because she wrote for a weekly paper, and the rules at the time only granted press credentials to daily reporters. Six months later, she became the first Black female reporter to earn Congressional press credentials, but it wasn't easy for her. She wasn't allowed into many of the proceedings at the White House because she was Black. President Eisenhower refused to answer her questions at first, and then made her submit her questions in advance because she asked tough questions, often about race. At a senator's funeral, she was forced to sit in the servants' section to cover the event. In 1947, she was named bureau chief of the **Associated Negro Press**. She held this position for fourteen years. In 1948, Alice was one of three Black reporters who covered Harry S. Truman's presidential campaign. She paid her own way to

Words You Should Know

» The House of Representatives is one of the two parts of the Congress of the United States. There are currently 435 representatives in the House. They represent districts in their home states and serve a two-year term.

» The Senate is one of the two parts of Congress. There are currently one hundred senators serving in the senate. Each senator serves a six-year term. Each state elects two senators to represent it in Congress.

follow him on the campaign trail. In 1948, she also became the first Black female White House correspondent, and was the first Black woman elected to the Women's National Press Club. She traveled all over the world as a reporter, to places like Canada, Israel, Mexico, South America, Africa, and the Caribbean. In 1960, Dunnigan left the press to work in the White House for the Kennedy Administration as an education consultant for the president's Committee on Equal Opportunity. She stayed in the White House through President Johnson's administration, but retired when Richard Nixon was elected in 1968.

Words You Should Know

» A White House correspondent is a journalist who covers news from the White House and reports on the president. They attend presidential briefings and report on happenings in the White House.

After her time in the White House, Alice went back to writing, but this time, she wrote her autobiography *A Black Woman's Experience: From Schoolhouse to White House*. She also wrote a book about the history of Black Kentuckians. She died in 1983

Here are some wise words to remember Alice by: "Without black writers, the world would perhaps never have known of the chicanery, shenanigans, and buffoonery employed by those in high places to keep the black man in his (proverbial) place by relegating him to second-class citizenship."

A is for Alice

Kentucky
Central Kentucky, home of the bluegrass region of the state, was home to the most slaveholders prior to the Civil War. Kentucky largely remained split between Union and Confederate sympathizers during the war, and never really took part in any of the major battles of the Civil War, choosing to remain neutral. During their slaveholding days, Kentucky slaves grew tobacco and hemp, and were known for their prize livestock. Kentucky was the fifteenth state admitted to the Union when it split off from Virginia in 1792.

World War II
During World War II, more than 2.5 million Black American men registered for the draft and many Black women volunteered for service. Altogether, more than one million Black servicemen served during World War II.

Howard University
Howard University is a historically Black college that was founded in 1867. It offers undergraduate, graduate, and professional degree programs in more than 120 disciplines, more than any other historically Black College in the nation. Howard is also distinct in that it has always allowed students of all races and genders to attend its school.

Black-owned newspaper
Freedom's Journal is the oldest Black-owned newspaper in the United States. It was founded by Reverend Peter Jones Jr. and other free Black men in New York City in 1827. It published a four-page, four-column edition weekly.

Associated Negro Press
The Associated Negro Press was founded in 1919 in Chicago, Illinois, and ran until 1967. It was founded by Claude Albert Barnett. The Associated Negro Press provided news relevant to Black Americans at first, but later became a global network of news reporters who would submit their stories for syndication in Black-owned newspapers.

Committee on Equal Opportunity
The Committee on Equal Opportunity was established after an executive action was signed by President John F. Kennedy that mandated that government contractors "take affirmative action to ensure that applicants are employed and that employees are treated during employment without regard to their race, creed, color, or national origin."

Black Kentuckians
Black Kentuckians have had a long history of greatness in the state. From sports legends to advocates for the mentally ill, Kentucky has no shortage of great Black figures. To discover more about Black Kentuckians and their history, you can check out the Black Kentucky Hall of Fame at: https://kchr.ky.gov/Hall-of-Fame/Pages/Gallery-of-Great-Black-Kentuckians.aspx

Bessie Coleman

essie Coleman was a Black and Native American aviator. She was born in 1892 in Atlanta, Texas. On her father's side of the family, her grandparents were Cherokee, and her mother was Black. Bessie was the tenth of thirteen children. Her family were sharecroppers. They moved to Waxahachie, Texas, when she was two years old. Bessie walked four miles to school each day to a one-room segregated schoolhouse where she was an excellent student, especially in mathematics. Every year, during the cotton harvest, Bessie had to leave school to work the fields with her family. Her father returned to Indian territory and left his family behind. When she was twelve, Bessie was accepted into the Missionary Baptist Church school on a scholarship. When she graduated high school, she went to the Oklahoma Colored Agricultural and Normal University in Langston, Oklahoma, but she had to drop out when she ran out of savings after just one term.

When she was twenty-three, she moved to Chicago and lived with her brothers while working as a manicurist. She heard stories about pilots returning from World War I and became determined to learn how to fly, but at the time, no Blacks or women were allowed to obtain pilot's licenses in the United States. Bessie took a second job to save up money to study aviation overseas. Robert Abbott, the founder and publisher of a Black newspaper, the

Words You Should Know

» An aviator is someone who flies an aircraft.

» A manicurist is someone who cleans and decorates fingernails.

» Aviation is the operation of aircrafts.

Chicago Defender, publicized her quest in his newspaper, and she received funding from the paper and a banker to study in France. On June 15, 1921, Bessie became the first Black American and the first Native American to earn a pilot's license. People weren't yet traveling much by plane, so in order to make a living as a pilot, Bessie had to learn **trick flying** and perform stunts at exhibition flights and airshows. She was a popular stunt pilot and drew big crowds, and she used her popularity to speak out against racism. She refused to fly in any show where Black people were not allowed to attend. Bessie died in a plane crash in 1926.

Words You Should Know

» A stunt pilot is a person who performs aerobatic maneuvers or trick flying with their aircraft.

Here are some wise words to remember Bessie by: "The air is the only place free from prejudice."

B is for Bessie

Interesting Facts

Cherokee

The Cherokee developed their own alphabet and adopted many of the white man's ways, including slaveholding. They were still forced to march from their homes in Georgia and the Carolinas along the Trail of Tears to Oklahoma, where they were placed on reservation land. The Cherokee brought their slaves with them on the Trail of Tears. Many died during the journey.

Waxahachie, Texas

Waxahachie, Texas, has a long history of segregation and discrimination. This became news in 2020 when it was discovered that the town's only Black elected official, Constable Curtis Polk Jr. was forced to use a basement stairwell as his office. Next to his desk hung a sign that read "Negros." After a public outcry, Polk's office was moved and the judge who had ordered him to the stairwell office was investigated for vandalism.

Segregated schoolhouse

During much of the 1700s to early 1900s, students were taught in one-room schoolhouses in rural areas. A one-room segregated schoolhouse meant that only Black children could attend. Segregated schoolhouses came into being after the Civil War, when Black people were given the rights to read and write. Prior to the Civil War, it was illegal in most slave states for Black people to read or write. Black schools often had fewer resources than white schools.

Trick flying
Also called aerobatic maneuvers, trick flying is when a pilot performs tricks with his or her aircraft, such as spins, dives, loops, and rolls. It can be very dangerous to perform these tricks.

Charles Hamilton Houston

Charles Hamilton Houston was a prominent Black lawyer, dean of Howard Law School, and an important civil rights attorney. Charles was born in Washington, DC, in 1895. His father was a lawyer and the son of a former slave, and his mother was a seamstress. Charles attended segregated local schools and entered Amherst College when he graduated high school. After graduating in 1915 as valedictorian and the only Black student in his class, he took a job teaching English at Howard University. When World War I broke out, Charles joined the Army as an officer. While in the military, he became determined to go to school to study law to fight back against the discrimination he faced in the military, which was still segregated at that time. When he returned to the United States from **France**, where he'd been stationed during the war, he entered Harvard Law School. He was the first Black student to work on the editorial board of the *Harvard Law Review*.

> ## Words You Should Know
>
> » A valedictorian is the top student in her or his class. They have the highest grade point average.

In 1924, he was admitted to the Washington, DC bar and joined his father's practice. He was recruited to the Howard University Law School by the school's first Black president, Mordecai Johnson. While at Howard, he served as the Vice Dean and Dean of the law school. He taught his students that the law could be used to fight racial discrimination and encouraged them to use it to fight injustice.Among his students was Thurgood Marshall, who later became a Supreme Court justice. In 1935, Charles left Howard to serve as the first special counsel for the NAACP. Through his work at the NAACP, he argued or took part in many important civil rights cases. In particular, he argued for an end to discriminatory housing practices and against Jim Crow laws that kept Black people segregated from whites. He died in 1950.

Words You Should Know

» The National Association for the Advancement of Colored People, or NAACP, is a nationwide organization that fights for equality for Black people. It was founded in 1909 in New York City.

» Jim Crow laws were laws that were specifically written to keep Black people separate from white people. For example, under Jim Crow laws, Black people had to use separate toilet facilities, sit at separate lunch counters, and drink from different water fountains. These laws also prevented Black people from equally accessing education and the right to vote.

Here are some wise words to remember Charles by: "The race problem in the United States is the type of unpleasant problem which we would rather do without but which refuses to be buried."

C is for Charles

Interesting Facts

France

During World Wars I and II, many Black American soldiers went to France on breaks from their combat duties. In France, they were not segregated or discriminated against. Many Black American performers also traveled to France to perform, so the culture was welcoming to the Black soldiers.

Supreme Court

The Supreme Court is one of the three main branches of government, along with Congress and the Executive Branch (presidency). The Supreme Court is the highest court in the land and has final say in many arguments that are brought before them. Thurgood Marshall was the first Black Supreme Court Justice. Supreme Court Justices serve life terms.

Daisy Bates

Daisy Bates was a civil rights activist, publisher, journalist, and lecturer. She was born in 1914 in Arkansas. When she was just three years old, her mother was murdered by three white men who were never brought to justice. This made Daisy angry about racial injustice from an early age. She was raised by adoptive parents. She attended segregated schools in Huttig, Arkansas, which further angered her because the schools were not as well-equipped as white schools in the area. In 1941, she married L. C. Bates, a former journalist and insurance salesman. Shortly after their marriage, they moved to Little Rock, Arkansas, and launched the *Arkansas State Press*, a newspaper dedicated to reporting on civil rights issues and police brutality against Black citizens in Arkansas.

Daisy was selected to serve as the president of the NAACP's Arkansas branch in 1952. After the US Supreme Court declared that segregation was unconstitutional in 1954, Daisy led the NAACP's protest against Little Rock's plans for a gradual integration of the schools, pressing instead for immediate integration. She would take Black children to predominantly white schools to enroll them, accompanied by newspaper photographers who documented when the schools would not allow them to attend. This put pressure on the school district to integrate quickly. Despite a court order, Bates and nine Black students were denied entry to Central High School. Finally, on September 27, 1957, President Dwight D. Eisenhower ordered all Arkansas National Guardsmen and a thousand paratroopers to enforce integration at the school, and Daisy and the nine students were escorted into the school safely. Daisy continued to speak out for the students during their time at Central High School.

In 1962, Daisy published her autobiography, *The Long Shadow of Little Rock*. She worked for President Lyndon Johnson's anti-poverty program for a few years and was a noted public speaker and community activist. She died in 1999.

Here are some wise words to remember Daisy by: "No man or woman who tries to pursue an ideal in his or her own way is without enemies."

D is for Daisy

Interesting Facts

Arkansas

Arkansas was part of the Louisiana Purchase and joined the union as its twenty-fifth state in 1835. Much of the state had been developed for cotton production, and Arkansas relied heavily on slave labor to keep its cotton plantations running. Arkansas left the Union during the Civil War, but even after rejoining the Union, it struggled because of its overreliance on cotton and a plantation economy. Arkansas was the site of several battles during the civil rights movement, especially over school integration.

Little Rock

Little Rock is the capital and most populous city in Arkansas. It was central to the struggle to integrate the school system in the 1950s, and Daisy Bates was a central figure in the struggle to see the schools integrated.

The Long Shadow of Little Rock

Daisy Bates's memoir about her role in the struggle to integrate Arkansas public schools was banned in the South for years. After the University of Arkansas Press reprinted the book in 1988, it won an American Book Award. It tells the story of how President Dwight Eisenhower sent federal troops to integrate the public schools in Arkansas, the first time in eighty-one years that a president had sent federal troops to protect the rights of Black Americans.

Eartha Kitt

Eartha Kitt was a singer, actress, dancer, comedienne, author, activist, and songwriter. She was born on a cotton plantation in South Carolina in 1927. Her mother was Cherokee and Black. She did not know who her father was. Eartha was bullied from a young age because of her mixed-race heritage. Her mother gave her away and sent her to live with an aunt in Harlem, New York. On a friend's dare, she tried out for the Katherine Dunham Dance Company and won a spot as a dancer and singer while she was still a teenager. Eartha toured worldwide with the dance company and was spotted by a Paris nightclub owner, who booked her as a featured singer. Her unique charm and personality gained her fame quickly.

Back in New York, she performed on Broadway and began earning film roles and recording contracts. Orson Welles called her "the most exciting woman in the world." During her early years in show business, she published her first autobiography, *Thursday's Child.* She could sing in ten languages and toured in over one hundred countries. In 1967, she played Catwoman on the television series *Batman,* and was an instant sensation in the role. But, in 1968, while at a luncheon at the White House, hosted by Lady Bird Johnson, Eartha spoke out against the Vietnam War, and was blacklisted in the United States, where no one would hire her to perform. She was forced to live overseas for many years. In 1974, she returned to the United States for an acclaimed Carnegie Hall concert. She published three more books, and earned Tony and Grammy nominations for her performing arts work.

Eartha was also a busy activist. She founded the Kittsville Youth Foundation, which helped underprivileged children in the Watts section of Los Angeles. She was an anti-war activist and spoke out against the war in Vietnam, and was a supporter of LGBTQ rights, including marriage equality. Eartha died in 2008.

Here are some wise words to remember Eartha by: "My recipe for life is not being afraid of myself, afraid of what I think or of my opinions."

Words You Should Know

» **Marriage equality** is the policy that any two people should be able to marry regardless of sexual orientation or gender. In 2015, the Supreme Court decided that all same-sex marriages must be legally recognized in the United States.

E is for Eartha

Interesting Facts

South Carolina

South Carolina was the eighth state to enter the union in 1788. By the 1800 census, the state population was nearly 340,000, of whom 146,000 were slaves. South Carolina relied heavily on the cotton plantation, and many of its landowners kept slaves. During the Civil War, however, many white planters fled South Carolina, leaving tens of thousands of slaves behind. The Union Forces freed these slaves, and several charities worked with the former slaves to help them run the cotton plantations. They were paid for every pound of cotton they picked. This made them the first slaves freed by Union forces and the first freed slaves to earn a wage.

The Katherine Dunham Dance Company

The Katherine Dunham Dance Company was founded in 1930 by Katherine Dunham. It was the first Black American modern dance company. Starting in the 1940s, the group went on several successful world tours and launched the careers of Eartha Kitt, Alvin Ailey, Rosalie King, Frances Davis, and Walter Nicks.

Broadway

Broadway, or Broadway Theatre, is a group of forty-one professional theatres located in New York City in Midtown Manhattan. Broadway is considered the center of American theatre.

Orson Welles

Orson Welles was an actor, director, screenwriter, and producer. He is considered one of the greatest filmmakers of all time. He was born in 1915. When he was in his twenties, he directed an all-Black adaptation of Shakespeare's *Macbeth* for the Federal Theatre Project.

Vietnam War

The Vietnam War was fought over South Vietnam's desire to remain a democracy and North Vietnam's desire to become a communist country. At the time of the war, the United States was afraid that communism was spreading too quickly in Southeast Asia, and sent troops and equipment to help the South Vietnamese. Three hundred thousand Black soldiers served in Vietnam.

Fritz Pollard

Fritz Pollard was a professional football player and coach. He was born in 1927 in **Chicago, Illinois**. He attended Albert G. Lane Manual Training School in Chicago, where he was on the football, baseball, and track teams. After high school, he attended Brown University, where he studied chemistry. He was the first Black player on Brown's football team, and the first Black running back to be selected for Walter Camp's All-America Team. From 1918 to 1920, Fritz coached Lincoln University's football team. Along with Bobby Marshall, Fritz was one of the first two Black players in the NFL in 1920, when he joined the Akron Pros as a running back. In 1921, he was co-head coach of the Akron Pros, while still playing as a running back on the team. He also played for the Milwaukee Badgers, the Hammond Pros, the Gilberton Cadamounts, the Union Club of Phoenixville, and the Providence Steam Roller. In 1926, Pollard and all nine of the **Black NFL players** were removed from the league. They never returned. In the 1930s, Fritz founded his own pro football team, the **Brown Bombers**. Later in life, he became a tax consultant, talent agent, and film and music producer. He also published the *New York Independent News*, a newspaper, from 1935 to 1942. He was inducted into the **Pro Football Hall of Fame** in 2005. Fritz died in 1986.

Here are some wise words to remember Fritz by: "The ball is your life, if you drop it, that's a different story."

F is for Fritz

Chicago, Illinois

Chicago, Illinois, is the third most populous city in the United States. It was founded in the 1780s by Jean Baptiste Point du Sable, a Haitian explorer. Chicago was the destination of many Black Americans during the Great Migration after the Civil War, when former slaves wanted to leave the South and Jim Crow laws.

Black NFL Players

The first Black professional football player is believed to be Charles Follis, who played for the Shelby Steamfitters from 1902 to 1906. In the very early days of the sport, there were very few Black professional football players. Between 1920 and 1926, there were only nine Black players in total. They were commonly the first players let go when the teams changed their playing lineups. In contrast, other ethnic minorities were more common in the sport, including many Native Americans. Black players found themselves locked out of football for many years; between 1934 and the end of World War II, there were no Black professional football players at all. After World War II, things began to slowly change, and more and more Black players were drafted to play for the NFL. In 2014, a survey of players found that 68.7 percent of the professional football players were Black Americans.

Brown Bombers

The Brown Bombers were an all-Black football team from Harlem, New York. They were founded in the summer of 1935 by Herschel Day, a Black athletic promoter. At the time of their founding, the NFL was refusing to draft Black players for their teams, and their coach, Fritz Pollard, wanted to prove that Black players could successfully play a game against white players with no racial incidents. They played in several exhibition games against professional football teams and had a good record of winning many of the games. The problem that the Brown Bombers faced was that they didn't receive media coverage, except in Black-owned newspapers, and couldn't draw a large enough crowd to cover the players' salaries. In addition, very few professional teams were willing to play the all-Black Bombers.

Pro Football Hall of Fame

The Pro Football Hall of Fame was founded in 1963. It is located in Canton, Ohio, and is affiliated with the Black College Football Hall of Fame. The Hall of Fame receives visitors from all fifty states and several foreign nations every year.

Guion Bluford Jr.

Guion Bluford Jr. is an aerospace engineer, a retired astronaut, and a former **Air Force** officer and pilot. He was the first Black American to go to space. Guion was born in **Philadelphia, Pennsylvania**, in 1942. He earned a Bachelor of Science degree in Aerospace Engineering from Pennsylvania State University in 1960, and a Master of Science degree and then a PhD from the US Air Force Institute of Technology. In 1964, he joined the Air Force, where he trained as a fighter pilot. He flew 144 combat missions during the Vietnam War. Guion was selected from over ten thousand applicants to be

Words You Should Know

» **Aerospace engineers** design aircraft, spacecraft, satellites, and missiles.

one of thirty-five astronauts to receive training to fly on the Space Shuttle. On August 30, 1983, he rode the Orbiter *Challenger* into orbit to deploy a communications satellite. He was in space until September 5, 1983, when the *Challenger* returned successfully to Earth. On his next mission, he and five other astronauts flew to Spacelab and performed more than seventy experiments. On his next mission into space, which launched April 28, 1991, he conducted experiments to study the atmosphere and the environment inside the space shuttle. He also released a satellite from the space shuttle's cargo bay. On his final mission into space aboard the space shuttle *Discovery*, he released a military communications satellite. In all, Guion spent twenty-eight days in space! Guion retired from **NASA** in 1987.

Here are some wise words to remember Guion by: "I felt an awesome responsibility, and I took the responsibility very seriously, of being a role model and opening another door to black Americans, but the important thing is not that I am black, but that I did a good job as a scientist and an astronaut. There will be black astronauts flying in later missions...and they, too, will be people who excel, not simply who are black... who can ably represent their people, their communities, their country."

G is for Guion

Interesting Facts

Air Force
The US Air Force was initially formed as part of the US Army in 1907. It became a separate branch of the armed services in 1947. More than 329,000 active-duty personnel are part of the US Air Force, but only about 6 percent of all officers in the Air Force are Black.

Philadelphia, Pennsylvania
Philadelphia, Pennsylvania, is the most populous city in the state of Pennsylvania. It was founded in 1682 by William Penn to serve as the capital of the colony of Pennsylvania. Philadelphia was an important city in the founding of the United States. The Declaration of Independence was signed in Philadelphia. It was a meeting place for the Founding Fathers of the United States and is home to the Liberty Bell. Philadelphia was a safe place for slaves escaping the South prior to the Civil War, and after the Civil War, during the Great Migration, it was the chosen destination of many freed slaves who wished to leave the South and Jim Crow laws.

Challenger
The Orbiter *Challenger* was the second of NASA's space shuttles. It flew its first mission on April 4, 1983. The *Challenger* flew nine missions before an explosion destroyed it on January 28, 1986. On that flight, seventy-three seconds after takeoff, the space shuttle exploded and disintegrated, killing all seven crew members and a civilian teacher who was on the flight.

NASA

NASA, the National Aeronautics and Space Administration, is an agency that is responsible for the civilian space program. It also conducts aeronautical and space research. It was established in 1958 and grew out of the National Advisory Committee for Aeronautics.

Henrietta Lacks

Henrietta Lacks was a housewife and tobacco farmer whose cancer cells are the source of the first immortalized cancer cell line, and whose cells continue to be used for research. Henrietta was born in Roanoke, Virginia, in 1920. When she was four years old, her mother died giving birth to her tenth child, and the family was split up. Henrietta was sent to live with her maternal grandfather in Clover, Virginia, where she began farming tobacco at a young age to help support her family. She was married in 1951 and had five children. Shortly after she was married, her family moved to Turner Station, Maryland, for better job opportunities. After giving birth to her last child, Henrietta was diagnosed with cervical cancer. Some of her cells were sent to a researcher, George Gey, at Johns Hopkins, without her permission. Dr. Gey discovered that Henrietta's cells were unlike any of the other cells he studied. The other cells would all die off quickly, but Henrietta's cells doubled every twenty to twenty-four hours. Henrietta's incredible immortal cells, named the "HeLa" line, have been used in medical research for many different things. They allow doctors to perform experiments without testing on humans and have been used to test the effects of toxins, drugs,

Words You Should Know

» Cervical cancer is a cancer of the cervix, which is an opening located at the mouth of the uterus in women. Today, cervical cancer is easily detectable with yearly tests.

» Toxins are harmful or poisonous substances produced within living cells or organisms. Toxins can cause disease.

Words You Should Know

» **Hormones** are substances produced by the body and transported through the blood or other liquid that signal tissues or specific cells to produce an action. For example, thyroid hormones are produced by the thyroid gland and help to regulate a person's metabolism.

hormones, and virus cells on cancer cells. They were also instrumental in developing the **polio** vaccine and studying the **human genome**. Although Henrietta Lacks died of cervical cancer in 1951, at the age of thirty-one, her life has saved many others.

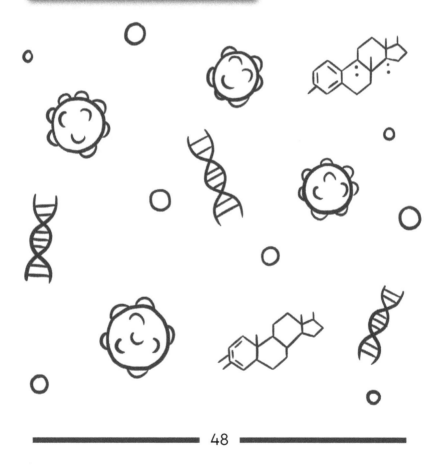

H is for Henrietta

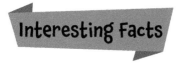

Interesting Facts

Immortal cells

Immortal cells are cells that have been engineered or have mutated to reproduce indefinitely. This makes it possible for doctors and other scientists to study the cells in the lab over a long period of time.

Polio

Polio, short for poliomyelitis, is an infectious disease. The effects of polio vary, but most people associate polio with weakness and paralysis of the muscles, which is a side effect that very rarely occurs. Polio has probably been around for thousands of years, but for most of its history, polio was a relatively rare disease. However, in the early 1900s, polio became much more active and more and more people, especially children, became infected with the disease. A polio vaccine was developed by Dr. Jonas Salk and was first used in 1955. Today, because of that vaccine, polio has mostly been defeated; however, some areas of Pakistan and Afghanistan still have outbreaks of the disease.

Human genome

The human genome is a complete set of all the DNA that people have. DNA is the blueprint that cells use to determine features of a person, for example, eye and skin color.
The human genome is a kind of map that scientists can use to study humans and diseases. Scientists announced that they had completed mapping the human genome in 2004.

Ida B. Wells-Barnett

Ida B. Wells-Barnett was a journalist, activist, and researcher. She was born into slavery in **Holly Springs, Mississippi**, in 1862, during the Civil War. Once the war ended, her family became active in Reconstruction politics. Her father became a trustee at Rust College, where Ida enrolled. In 1878, tragedy struck the Wells family, and both of Ida's parents and one of her brothers died during a **yellow fever** epidemic.

Ida was visiting her grandparents at the time and did not become ill. Ida was one of eight children in the family, and her relatives wanted to split the children up and send them to foster homes, but Ida refused. To keep the family together, she found work as a schoolteacher in Holly Springs, Mississippi. Her grandmother stayed with the children during the week while Ida was teaching at the school. She moved to **Memphis, Tennessee**, in 1883 with her siblings. She continued working there as a schoolteacher. In 1884, Ida sued a train company for throwing her off a first-class car, even though she had a ticket. She won the case in the local courts, but the verdict was overturned on appeal in federal court.

Words You Should Know

» **Yellow Fever** is a disease that is caused by an infection from diseased mosquitoes. Most people recover quickly from yellow fever, but in rare cases, the disease attacks the liver, which causes the skin of the infected person to turn yellow. There is a vaccine for yellow fever, which is still active in many warm areas of the world.

After one of her friends was lynched, Ida began to study the reasons why lynchings occurred, and produced a pamphlet with her findings and wrote columns in several newspapers. After she published an article about a lynching in 1892, locals became enraged and set her press on fire, driving her out of Memphis. She relocated to Chicago, Illinois. In 1893, Ida joined a boycott of the Columbian Exposition in Chicago because Black people were not allowed to attend and were negatively portrayed in the exposition. She married prominent Black attorney Ferdinand Barnett in 1895. Ida also traveled internationally, speaking out about lynchings. She openly confronted women in the women's voting rights movement for ignoring lynchings. Because of her beliefs, she was often criticized in women's rights circles, but she stayed active in women's rights causes anyway. She was a founder of the **National Association of Colored Women's Clubs**, which was founded to address concerns of women's rights and civil rights for Black people. She was present during the founding of the NAACP but is not listed as a founder. She died in 1931.

Here are some wise words to remember Ida by: "The way to right wrongs is to turn the light of truth upon them."

> ## Words You Should Know
>
> » A lynching is when a mob of people kill a person, usually by hanging, without a trial.

I is for Ida

Interesting Facts

Holly Springs, Mississippi

Holly Springs, Mississippi, is a city in Mississippi that is on the southern border of Tennessee. It was founded in 1836. As the area around Holly Springs grew, cotton plantations were built and depended on slave labor. Many of the slaves in Holly Springs were traded and separated from their families to meet the growing demand for slave labor. After the Civil War, many former slaves continued to farm cotton as sharecroppers for their former owners. In 1878, a yellow fever epidemic in Holly Springs killed three hundred people, including Ida's family members.

Memphis, Tennessee

Memphis is a city in Tennessee that sits on the Mississippi River. It was founded in 1819. Memphis has the largest population of Black Americans in Tennessee and was an important city during the civil rights era. Dr. Martin Luther King Jr. was assassinated in Memphis. It is home to the National Civil Rights Museum.

National Association of Colored Women's Clubs

The National Association of Colored Women's Clubs is an organization that was founded in 1896. It grew out of a need for Black women's groups to better communicate and coordinate with each other. Their motto is "lifting as we climb."

Joe Louis

Joe Louis was a professional boxer. He was born in 1914 in rural **Chambers County, Alabama**. Both of his parents were children of former slaves. His mother was half-Cherokee. Joe was the seventh of eight children born to his parents, who were sharecroppers and rental farmers. Growing up, Joe had a speech impediment, so he spoke very little until he was around six years old. Joe's father was committed to a mental institution in 1916, so he never really knew him. His mother remarried a local construction worker. In 1926, a local gang of **Ku Klux Klan** scared the family and they relocated to **Detroit, Michigan**, where Joe attended school and spent time at a local youth recreation center, where he learned to box. His mother wanted him to learn the violin instead of boxing, but Joe used the money she gave him for violin lessons to learn how to box. His debut fight was in 1932, when he was seventeen years old. He lost the fight to future Olympian boxer Johnny Miller. He continued boxing, winning several local **Golden Gloves** competitions. In April 1934, he won the United States Amateur Champion AAU Tournament. At the end of his amateur career, his record was 50 wins, 4 losses, and 43 knockouts.

Words You Should Know

» A speech impediment is a difficulty in speaking such as a lisp or a stutter.

» A mental institution is a long-term care facility or hospital for people with emotional and mental illnesses.

In 1937, Joe became the first Black heavyweight champion in twenty-two years when he beat James J. Braddock. Joe became an inspiration to Black Americans in the middle of the Great Depression, when Black people had a harder time finding and keeping work. Joe defended his title thirteen times between 1939 and 1941. His biggest fight may have been his match against German boxer Max Schmeling in 1938. At the time, World War II was in its early days, and Americans saw the match as symbolic of the struggle against Nazi Germany. Joe beat Max Schmeling in two minutes, four seconds, knocking him out in the first round in front of more than seventy thousand fans at Yankee Stadium in New York. During World War II, Joe donated almost $100,000 to Army and Navy causes. He joined the Army in 1942 and performed boxing exhibitions for service members all around the world. After eleven years and eight months as heavyweight champion, Joe retired from boxing in 1949. He later came out of retirement, in 1951, but was knocked out by Rocky Marciano. At the end of his professional career, Joe's record was 68 wins to 3 losses, and 54 knockouts. He died in 1981.

Here are some wise words to remember Joe by: "You need a lot of different types of people to make the world better."

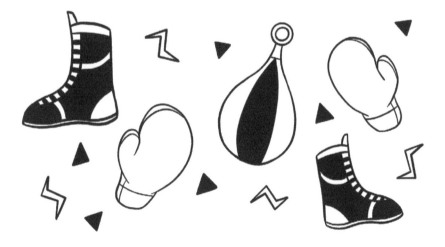

J is for Joe

Interesting Facts

Chambers County, Alabama

Chambers County, Alabama, was founded in 1832. It is named for Henry H. Chambers, who served as a senator from Alabama. Pat Garrett, who is famous for killing the outlaw Billy the Kid, was also born in Chambers County.

Ku Klux Klan

The Ku Klux Klan is a hate organization that targets Black people, Jewish people, immigrants, homosexuals, Catholics, Muslims, and atheists. They were founded in Pulaski, Tennessee, on December 24, 1865, by six former Confederate officers. The Klan is known for widespread violence and for dressing in hooded outfits. They often burn crosses on the front lawns of people they are targeting. Many lynchings have been the result of Klan activity. They embrace the idea of white supremacy, that is, that the white race is superior to all other races.

Detroit, Michigan

Detroit is the largest city in Michigan, and the largest city on the border with Canada. The city was founded in 1701. Also known as "Motor City," Detroit is home to several large automotive manufacturing plants. It has a large Black population and is known for its music and culture. Detroit was home to Motown music, and techno music developed there. It was also important in the development of jazz, hip-hop, rock and roll, and punk music.

Golden Gloves

Golden Gloves is the name given to several annual competitions for amateur boxers in the United States. The first Golden Gloves competition was held in 1928.

Great Depression

The Great Depression was a worldwide economic depression that lasted from 1929 until the late 1930s. A number of factors led to the Great Depression in the United States. The stock market collapsed in 1929, which led to a shortage of investors. In the United States, this was made worse by the Dust Bowl, a series of dust storms that ruined crops in the Great Plains and led to farmers losing their incomes. Unemployment in the United States rose to 23 percent, and many people could not find work to support themselves and their families. It was especially difficult for Black Americans during the Great Depression because they were "last hired, first fired," and had an especially hard time finding work that paid a living wage.

Army and Navy causes

There were several organizations during World War II that were dedicated to serving service men, but the best known is probably the USO, or United Service Organization. The USO was founded in 1941 to help raise the spirits of troops during World War II by providing them live entertainment, such as musicians, comedians, actors, and actresses. Many celebrities have participated in USO shows as a way of showing support and appreciation to the troops.

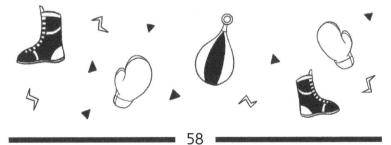

Kwame Ture

Kwame Ture was a civil rights activist. He was born in 1941 in Trinidad and Tobago, where his grandmother raised him until he was eleven. At that point, he reunited with his parents in New York City, where they had emigrated when he was two years old. Kwame attended the Bronx High School of Science, which was an elite school. There, he boycotted a local White Castle restaurant that refused to hire Black workers. In high school he also learned about the sit-ins that were happening in the South and joined the Congress of Racial Equality's protest against Woolworth's, which had segregated lunch counters.

In 1960, Kwame enrolled at Howard University as a philosophy major. While a student at Howard, he joined the Freedom Rides, which challenged racial segregation on interstate bus trips. He was arrested in Mississippi for protesting this segregation. Dr. Martin Luther King Jr.'s organization, the Southern Christian Leadership Conference, awarded Kwame a scholarship in response to his arrest. In the four years he was at Howard University, Kwame participated in many civil rights protests.

Words You Should Know

» A sit-in or sit-down is a form of protest used to protest segregation. During a sit-in, a group of people would occupy a place that was closed to them by Jim Crow laws, such as the lunch counter at Woolworth's. Sit-ins often provoked heckling and sometimes violence from people who were opposed to the protestors' message.

After graduating from Howard, in 1964, he joined the Student Nonviolent Coordinating Committee full time, where he worked on the **Mississippi Freedom Summer project**. In March 1965, he helped form the Lowndes County Freedom Organization in rural Alabama. This later became the **Black Panther Party**. In 1966, he took over from John Lewis as chairman of the Student Nonviolent Coordinating Committee. He coined the phrase "Black Power," and opposed the Vietnam War publicly. Kwame was Prime Minister of the Black Panther Party from 1967 to 1969. In 1969, he left the Black Panther Party and moved to **Guinea, Africa**, where he helped form the **All-African People's Revolutionary Party**. He died in 1998.

Here are some wise words to remember Kwame by: "The secret of life is to have no fear; it's the only way to function."

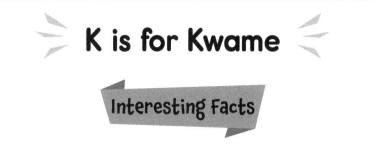

K is for Kwame

Interesting Facts

Trinidad and Tobago

Trinidad and Tobago are two islands in the south Caribbean Sea that together form the Republic of Trinidad and Tobago. The islands were inhabited by native tribes for many years, until Columbus arrived there in 1498 and claimed the islands as a Spanish colony. The islands changed rulers many times over the years, and they finally declared their independence in 1962. Trinidad and Tobago is a wealthy nation due to large reserves of oil and natural gas. The nation is known for its African and indigenous culture and holds a large Carnival festival every year. It is home to the steel pan drum and the limbo, and for music including calypso, soca, rapso, parang, chutney, and chutney soca.

New York City

New York City is the largest, most populous city in the United States, and the largest metropolitan area in the world. It was founded in 1624 by Dutch colonists. New York's Statue of Liberty stands in New York Harbor to welcome the many immigrants who come to the United States through New York each year. More languages are spoken in New York City than in any other place on the planet.

Freedom Rides

The Freedom Rides took place between May 4 and December 10, 1961. Freedom Riders were activists who rode interstate buses into the segregated Southern states to challenge the illegal segregation of buses. The Supreme Court had ruled that segregated busing was unconstitutional, but Southern police were not enforcing the ruling, and the buses were still segregated. Most of the Freedom Rides were sponsored by the Congress of Racial Equality, but the Student Nonviolent Coordinating Committee also helped organize some of them. The Freedom Riders were met with violence in several of the locations they rode to, including Birmingham, Alabama, Anniston, Alabama, and New Orleans, where they faced a bomb threat.

Mississippi Freedom Summer Project
Also known as Freedom Summer or the Mississippi Summer Project, the Mississippi Freedom Summer Project was a voter registration drive that took place in 1964, with the aim of increasing the number of Black registered voters in Mississippi. Over 700 mostly white volunteers traveled to Mississippi that summer and joined Black Mississippians to fight against voter discrimination. Several civil rights organizations, such as the Congress of Racial Equality and the Student Non-Violent Coordinating Committee, helped organize the summer project. The protestors met with violent resistance from local law enforcement and members of the Ku Klux Klan. The media coverage of the protests went global, sparking a backlash that led to the passage of the 1964 Civil Rights Act.

Black Panther Party
The Black Panther Party was a political organization founded by Bobby Seale and Huey P. Newton in 1966 in Oakland, California. The group officially disbanded in 1982. One of the party's first official activities was "copwatching," in which Black Panther members would carry loaded weapons and watch police in an effort to put a halt to police brutality. Eventually the Black Panthers developed a ten-point program aimed at

increasing Black power. They ran community soup kitchens, fed the needy, and supported other organizations that were fighting for social justice.

Guinea, Africa
The Republic of Guinea is along the west coast of Africa. French is the official language of Guinea. There are more than twenty-four ethnic groups in Guinea, and twenty-four languages are spoken there. Guinea was an important stop on the transatlantic slave trade route because it is a coastal nation. It was under French colonial rule from about 1898 to 1958. Today, Guinea is mostly a Muslim nation. About 85 percent of the country's population are Muslims.

All-African People's Revolutionary Party
The All-African People's Revolutionary Party is a political party founded by Kwame Nkrumah in 1968. Their aims include African unity, economic and technological advancement, and promoting the idea of African civilization and culture. The party has recruited members in more than thirty-three countries, including the United States, Canada, England, France, and many countries in the Caribbean and Africa.

Langston Hughes

Langston Hughes was an activist, poet, playwright, and novelist. He was born in 1902 in Joplin, Missouri. His parents divorced when he was still a young boy, and his father moved to Mexico. He was raised by his grandmother until he was thirteen, and then moved to Lincoln, Illinois, and later Cleveland, Ohio, with his mother and her second husband. He began writing poems while he was in Lincoln. When he was in high school, he was chosen to be class poet. His first published poem, "The Negro Speaks of Rivers," was published in the NAACP's magazine *The Crisis* in 1921.

After graduating from high school, Langston spent a year in Mexico, and then went to Columbia University for a year. He left Columbia because of racial prejudice against Black people from both students and teachers. He worked as a cook, launderer, and busboy to support himself during these years. He also took a job as a seaman and traveled to Africa and Europe. He lived for a time in Paris. Langston's first book of poetry, *The Weary Blues*, was published in 1926.

> ## Words You Should Know
>
> » A busboy is the person who clears tables after people eat in a restaurant or cafeteria.

He finished his college education in 1929 at Lincoln University in Pennsylvania. The year after he graduated from Lincoln, he published his first novel, *Not Without Laughter*. After graduating from college, Langston moved to Harlem, where he became a leading figure in the Harlem Renaissance. He later traveled to Russia and Spain, but mostly lived in Harlem for the rest of his life, where he continued to write about working-class Black people and their lives. He wrote memoir, operas, plays, poems, books for children, poetry, and essays. He died in 1967.

Here are some wise words to remember Langston by: "I have discovered in life that there are ways of getting almost anywhere you want to go, if you really want to go."

L is for Langston

Interesting Facts

Joplin, Missouri

Joplin is a city in southwestern Missouri. It was founded in 1873, after the Civil War ended. The area around Joplin was a frontier mining town. The main minerals that were mined there are zinc and lead. The city did well financially until the price of these minerals collapsed after World War II. During the Great Depression, the outlaws Bonnie and Clyde spent several weeks in Joplin and robbed several area businesses.

Cleveland, Ohio

Cleveland is a city in Ohio that is located on the southern shore of Lake Erie. It was founded in 1796. Cleveland was home to many active abolitionists prior to the Civil War, and was a major stop on the underground railroad for escaped slaves who were making their way to Canada across Lake Erie. Cleveland is home to the Rock and Roll Hall of Fame.

"The Negro Speaks of Rivers"

"The Negro Speaks of Rivers" is a poem written by Langston Hughes when he was seventeen years old. He wrote the poem while on his way to visit his father in Mexico. The poem uses rivers as a metaphor for the Black experience and for his own life. "The Negro Speaks of Rivers" is one of Langston Hughes's most famous poems. It was originally published in The Crisis in 1921.

The Weary Blues

The Weary Blues is both a poem by Langston Hughes and the title of his first collection of poetry. The poem was written in 1925 and first published in *Opportunity*, a publication of the Urban League, where it was awarded the magazine's prize for best poem of the year.

Not Without Laughter

Not Without Laughter is the title of Langston Hughes's debut novel. It was first published in 1930. The novel is about a group of Black people in Kansas and focuses on the effects of religion and class on people in the community. It is set in the 1910s.

Harlem Renaissance

The Harlem Renaissance was a movement that began in the early twentieth century, of cultural and artistic as well as economic growth in the neighborhood of Harlem in New York City. After the Civil War, during the Great Migration, many middle-class Black families moved to Harlem, and, starting about 1910 and lasting until the 1930s, there was an explosion of Black culture in the neighborhood that led to great works of literature, art, music, and stage performances. It also led to a change in culture, as many Black people were able to speak freely about their experiences for the first time, and they began organizing civil rights groups to change laws across the country.

Maya Angelou

Maya Angelou was a poet, memoirist, and civil rights activist. She was born in **St. Louis, Missouri**, in 1928. Her mother was a nurse and card dealer, and her father was a doorman and navy dietician. Maya's parents divorced when she was three years old, and she was sent to **Stamps, Arkansas**, to live with her grandmother, who owned a general store. She spent the next few years living between Stamps, Arkansas, and St. Louis, Missouri. When she was fourteen, she moved to **Oakland, California**, to live with her mother, who had moved west. When Maya was sixteen, she became the first Black streetcar conductor in San Francisco. In 1951, she began dancing in nightclubs in San Francisco and moved to New York to study **African dance**. During 1954 and 1955, Maya toured Europe, starring in a stage production of *Porgy and Bess*. Along the way, she recorded an album and began writing.

In 1960, she met Dr. Martin Luther King Jr. and began to organize for the Southern Christian Leadership Council (SCLC). She became the northern coordinator for the SCLC and helped them organize and raise money for the cause of civil rights. In 1961, Maya moved to **Cairo, Egypt**, where she became an associate editor at the weekly English-language newspaper the *Arab Observer*. From 1962 until 1965, Maya lived in **Accra, Ghana**, where she was an administrator at the University of

Words You Should Know

» A memoirist is a writer who writes stories about their own life from their own memories.

Ghana. In 1968, she wrote her first memoir, *I Know Why the Caged Bird Sings*. It was published in 1970.

Maya was a multi-talented woman. She produced television shows, acted, sang, and wrote articles, screenplays, documentaries, soundtracks, memoirs, and poetry. In 1981, she moved to North Carolina, where she taught a variety of subjects, including ethics, philosophy, science, theology, writing, and theatre at Wake Forest University. She toured the country and lectured widely. In 1993, Maya became the first Black inaugural poet when she recited her poem "On the Pulse of the Morning" at President Bill Clinton's inauguration. Maya died in 2014.

Words You Should Know

» **Theology** is the study of religion.

» An **inaugural poet** recites a poem at the presidential inauguration in Washington, DC. There have been six inaugural poets: Robert Frost, Maya Angelou, Miller Williams, Elizabeth Alexander, Richard Blanco, and Amanda Gorman. Maya was the second inaugural poet, and the first Black inaugural poet. She recited her poem "On the Pulse of the Morning" at President Bill Clinton's inauguration.

Here are some wise words to remember Maya by: "Love recognizes no barriers. It jumps hurdles, leaps fences, penetrates walls to arrive at its destination full of hope."

M is for Maya

Interesting Facts

St. Louis, Missouri
St. Louis is a city that sits on the Mississippi and Missouri Rivers. It was founded in 1764 by French fur traders and was later bought from France as part of the Louisiana Purchase. Lewis and Clark set off on their journey of discovery to explore the Louisiana Purchase Territory from St. Louis. Before the Civil War, St. Louis was a large slaveholding city. Many of the slaves worked on the waterfront and on riverboats. Many slaves escaped across the rivers into Illinois. During the Civil War, St. Louis suffered economically because the Union Army blocked river traffic south of the city which kept traders from getting through to the city.

Stamps, Arkansas
Stamps is a small town in rural Arkansas. A post office has been in the town since 1887. Stamps has a large percentage of Black Americans living in it. About 54 percent of the town is Black.

Oakland, California
Oakland is a city near San Francisco in California. It was incorporated in 1852. Many of the first settlers in Oakland were Chinese immigrants who had a difficult time settling there because they were discriminated against by white settlers. Several Chinese homes were burned in the 1850s. College students Bobby Seale and Huey Newton founded the Black Panther Party in Oakland.

African Dance

African dance is a style of dance that originated in sub-Saharan Africa. There are many cultures in Africa that use dance as part of their daily way of expressing themselves. The dances teach about social order and values and help people learn about different aspects of their culture, like history, poetry, and spirituality or religion. Dances are performed at funerals and festivals, and in most African dance there is no real separation between the dancers and those watching. Even spectators take part in the dances.

Cairo, Egypt

Cairo is the capital city of Egypt. It is located near the Nile River. Cairo is the sixth largest city in the world, and the second largest city in Africa. It was founded in 969 CE, but the area has been settled since very ancient times. The pyramids at Giza are located close to Cairo, and the city was a center of learning and art for many years. The library in Cairo held thousands of ancient texts. The world's second oldest university, Al-Azhar University, is located in Cairo.

Accra, Ghana

Accra is the capitol of Ghana, and has a population of about 4.2 million people. The city was settled in the fifteenth century. Accra was settled by many different groups of European traders. The Dutch, British, Swedes, Portuguese, Danish, and French all built forts in the area around what is now Accra. Accra is the most densely populated city in Ghana, and there are many industries in the city, including fishing, food manufacturing, lumber, textiles, clothing, and chemicals. Tourism is becoming more popular as well, as Accra has a thriving arts community, and the city is rich in history and culture.

I Know Why the Caged Bird Sings

I Know Why the Caged Bird Sings is the first of seven memoirs that Maya Angelou wrote. The book is written about her childhood from about the age of three until she became a mother at age sixteen. Maya was challenged to write the book by her friend, the author James Baldwin, who dared her to write an autobiography that was also a piece of literature. The book was nominated for the National Book Award and remained on the *New York Times* bestseller list for two years after it was published.

Nance Legins-Costley

Nance Legins-Costley was the first slave freed by Abraham Lincoln in 1841, twenty years before the Civil War, in a court case that went to the Illinois Supreme Court. She was born in 1813 in Kaskaskia, Illinois, into the household of Colonel Thomas Cox, who owned her parents despite Illinois being a free territory at that time. In 1827, Nance was sold to a man named Nathan Cromwell for $151, but she resisted being taken from the only household she had ever known and was locked in a windowless room for a week as punishment. She was then forced to go to her new home. Meanwhile, Colonel Cox tried to have the sale of his slaves reversed and took the case to court. Nance testified that she had not gone willingly to the new home and was not living there by her own choice. But the court decided she had no say in whether she was sold or not. The case went to appeal several times, and each time, Nance was declared a piece of property with no say over whether she could be bought and sold. When she was sold again to an abolitionist named David Bailey, a relative of Nathan Cromwell's went to court to try to take possession of her. David Bailey hired Abraham Lincoln to argue Nance's case before the Illinois Supreme Court and he won the case, arguing that, since every person in the state of Illinois was free regardless of color, no one could be bought or sold. Nance was freed! She lived the rest of her life in a log cabin in Pekin, Illinois, with her husband and children. She died in 1892.

N is for Nance

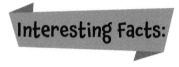

Interesting Facts:

Kaskaskia, Illinois

Kaskaskia is a village in Illinois. It had a population of fourteen residents according to the 2010 census. The population of Kaskaskia peaked in the eighteenth century at about seven thousand residents when it was a center for the British during the Revolutionary War.

Abraham Lincoln

Abraham Lincoln was a lawyer who served as the sixteenth president of the United States. He was born in a log cabin near Hodgenville, Kentucky, in 1809. Lincoln grew up in poverty and was self-educated. He became a lawyer in 1836, and was a member of the Whig party. He was elected to the Illinois state legislature in 1834, to the US House of Representatives in 1847, and was elected president of the United States in 1860. Lincoln was president during the Civil War and signed the Emancipation Proclamation, which freed the slaves, in 1863. He was assassinated by John Wilkes Booth in 1865.

Oscar Micheaux

Oscar Micheaux was an author and filmmaker. He was born in 1884 on a farm in Metropolis, Illinois. Oscar was the fifth of thirteen children, and his father had been born into slavery in Kentucky. Oscar's family moved to the city so that their children could get an education, but they ran into money troubles and had to return to the farm just a couple of years after moving away. When he was seventeen, Oscar moved to Chicago to live with one of his older brothers. He worked odd jobs to try to support himself. After he was cheated out of $2 by an employment agency, he decided to become his own boss and set up a shoeshine stand. He then became a Pullman porter on the railroads, which was considered a good job for Black people at the time, because it was stable and paid well. Oscar worked hard, met wealthy people, traveled all over the United States, and saved his money. When he had enough money, he moved to South Dakota, where he bought land and worked as a homesteader.

While farming, Oscar began writing articles and stories. After a few years, he decided to concentrate on writing. He wrote seven novels. His first book, *The Conquest: The Story of a Negro Pioneer*, sold a thousand copies. In 1918, his novel *The Homesteader* gained the attention of the Lincoln Motion Picture Company, a Black film company. Oscar tried to negotiate a contract to have the book made into a film, but when the deal fell through, he didn't give up. He started his own film company, Micheaux Film & Book Company. He went on to write, direct, film, and produce more than forty full-length motion pictures, both silent and with sound. At the time, filmmaking was a new industry, and most of the filmmakers were white. Oscar's films were met with commercial and critical success. He dealt directly with the racial issues of the time and showed his audience films that were accurate to a Black man's experience in America at the time. Oscar died in 1951.

Here are some wise words to remember Oscar by: "One of the greatest tasks of my life has been to teach the colored man he can be anything."

O is for Oscar

Interesting Facts

Metropolis, Illinois

Metropolis is a city located on the Ohio River in Illinois. It was founded in 1839. The city was settled by many people who moved north from slave states and brought their slaves with them. Even after Illinois was admitted to the union as a free state, many slaveowners kept slaves in Metropolis. Metropolis is also the hometown of Superman. There is a fifteen-foot-tall bronze statue of Superman in the city, and it is home to the Superman Museum.

P. B. S. Pinchback

P.B.S. **Pinchback** was the first Black governor of a state in the United States. He was born in 1837 in Macon, Georgia. His father was a white planter, and his mother was a former slave of his father's. Despite having a white family, P. B. S.'s father raised his half-Black children as he did his white children. When he was nine years old, P. B. S. was sent to Ohio to get an education. While he was in Ohio, his father died. His mother, fearing that relatives would try to enslave her and her children, fled north to Cincinnati, Ohio. When he was twenty-three, he married a free woman of color and moved to New Orleans. During the Civil War, P. B. S. fought on the side of the Union and was one of the Union's few Black commissioned officers, but he was passed over twice for promotion and left the Union Army in 1863. After the war, P. B. S. became active in politics, and in 1868 was elected as a Louisiana state senator. In 1871, when the lieutenant governor of Louisiana died, P. B. S. took over his position. In 1872, the legislature filed charges against the governor of Louisiana, Henry Clay Warmouth. P. B. S. stepped in as acting governor for the six weeks it took to impeach Warmouth, making him the first and only Black governor of a

Words You Should Know

» The US Marshals Service is the oldest federal law enforcement agency in the United States. They enforce the federal court system. US Marshals duties include protecting the federal courts, arresting federal fugitives, and housing and transporting federal prisoners.

state until 1989. He helped establish Southern University in 1880. In 1885, P. B. S. studied law at Straight University and was admitted to the bar, but never practiced. He moved with his family to Washington, DC, in 1892, and later worked as a US Marshal in New York. He died in 1921.

Here are some wise words to remember P.B.S by: "I am groping about through this American forest of prejudice and proscription, determined to find some form of civilization where all men will be accepted for what they are worth."

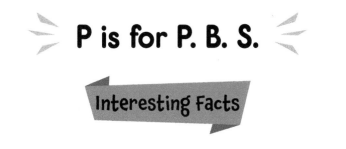

P is for P. B. S.

Interesting Facts

Macon, Georgia

Macon is a city in central Georgia. Its nickname is "The Heart of Georgia." It was settled in 1809 by traders who built a fort to trade with the local Native American population. The city was thriving in the years before the Civil War because it is located on the Ocmulgee River, which makes it convenient for trade. Cotton was the major crop in Macon prior to the Civil War, and the cotton plantations relied on slave labor to function. During the Civil War, Macon was the site of the Confederacy's arsenal and manufactured bullets and other weaponry. There was a prison camp located in Macon during the war that held up to 2,300 Union soldiers. Today, about 67 percent of the people who live in Macon are Black.

Cincinnati, Ohio

Cincinnati is a city in southwestern Ohio on the border with Kentucky. It was settled in 1788. Ohio was a free state before and during the Civil War. Cincinnati's location on the border with Kentucky, a slave state, made it a prime stop on the Underground Railroad, and many abolitionists lived in Cincinnati. Construction of the National Underground Railroad Freedom Center was finished in 2004 and serves as a museum of the Underground Railroad's history. It is located on Freedom Way in Cincinnati.

New Orleans

New Orleans is the largest city in Louisiana. It is located along the Mississippi River. It was founded in 1718 by French colonists and was once the capital of French Louisiana, before it was purchased by the United States in the Louisiana Purchase in 1803. New Orleans was home to the largest slave market in the nation prior to the Civil War. The city has a rich culture and is known for its Cajun and Creole cuisines, for jazz music, and for the annual Mardi Gras celebration.

Black Commissioned Officers

During the Civil War, about 179,000 Black men served as soldiers in the Union Army. About 19,000 Black sailors served in the Union Navy. About 40,000 Black soldiers and sailors died during the Civil War. Most of them, about 30,000, died of infections or diseases. Of all the Black soldiers and sailors during the Civil War, only about eighty were commissioned as officers, meaning they held a command position in the military.

Queen Latifah

Queen Latifah is a singer, songwriter, rapper, actress, and producer. She was born in **Newark, New Jersey**, in 1970. She grew up nearby in East Orange, New Jersey. Her mother was a schoolteacher, and her father was a policeman. They divorced when she was ten years old. Latifah graduated from Irvington High School and then took some courses at Borough of Manhattan Community College. In 1992, Latifah's older brother Lancelot Jr. died in an accident while driving a motorcycle Latifah had purchased for him. This led her into a period of drug abuse and depression from which she later recovered.

Latifah started her musical career by beatboxing for the hip-hop group Ladies Fresh. She has built a long career of rapping about issues important to Black women, such as domestic violence, relationship problems, and harassment. Her debut album *All Hail the Queen* was released in 1989 and featured the hit single "Ladies First." Her third album, *Black Reign*, won a Grammy Award. Latifah is also an actress. She had a starring role on the FOX Network television show *Living Single* from 1993 to 1998, and has starred in many films, including *Bringing Down the House, Taxi, Barbershop 2: Back in Business, Beauty Shop, Last Holiday, Hairspray, Joyful Noise,* and *22 Jump Street*, among others. Latifah has won a Grammy Award, an Emmy Award, a Golden Globe Award, three Screen Actors Guild Awards, two **NAACP Image Awards**, and has been nominated for an Academy Award. Latifah is the first hip-hop artist to receive a star on the **Hollywood Walk of Fame**.

Here are some wise words to remember Queen Latifah by: "Look at people for an example, but then make sure to do things your way. Surround yourself with positive people."

Q is for Queen

Interesting Facts

Newark, New Jersey

Newark is the most populous city in the state of New Jersey. It was settled in 1666 by Puritans, making it one of the oldest cities in the United States. According to the 2010 census, Newark has a 52.4 percent Black population. It is home to several large companies, including Panasonic, Audible.com, IDT Corporation, and Manischewitz. There are also several large universities in Newark, including Rutgers University, the New Jersey Institute of Technology, and Seton Hall University's Law School. Newark is an important city because it is located on the Passaic River and has easy access to New York Harbor, so it is a major shipping destination for the United States.

NAACP Image Awards

The NAACP Image Awards are given to Black entertainers for excellence in film, television, theatre, music, and literature. The award is sponsored by the National Association for the Advancement of Colored People. The first NAACP Image Awards were presented in 1967.

Hollywood Walk of Fame

The Hollywood Walk of Fame is a tourist attraction located in Hollywood, California. Over 2,600 brass five-pointed stars are embedded in the sidewalk along several city streets in Hollywood. The stars represent notable figures in the entertainment industry. The Walk of Fame was started in 1956. Stars for the Walk of Fame are nominated by committee.

Rebecca Lee Crumpler

Dr. **Rebecca Lee Crumpler** was a nurse, physician, and author. She was born in 1831 in Christiana, Delaware, but was raised by an aunt in Pennsylvania. Her aunt took care of the sick townspeople, and this had a big effect on Rebecca, who decided from an early age that she wanted to heal people who were sick. Rebecca moved to Charlestown, Massachusetts, where she worked as a nurse from 1855 to 1864, but this wasn't enough for her. She wanted to be a doctor and applied to the New England Female Medical College in 1860. Prior to 1860, it was rare for Black men or women to be accepted into medical schools, but the heavy fighting during the Civil War meant that doctors were needed, and Rebecca was accepted into the school with a scholarship. She was the only Black woman in the country studying medicine, and when she received her degree, she became the first Black female physician in the United States.

Rebecca practiced medicine in Boston, Massachusetts, where most of her patients were poor and Black. After the Civil War, she moved south to Richmond, Virginia, where she worked for the Freedmen's Bureau, providing medical care for freed slaves who were turned away by white doctors. Rebecca had a hard time at her job. People made fun of her and said the "MD" after her name stood for "Mule Driver," and many pharmacists refused to fill her prescriptions because she was Black. Rebecca moved back to Boston in the late 1860s, where she continued to treat Black patients. In 1883, she published a book called *A Book of Medical Discourses*, which talks about illnesses in young children and women. Rebecca died in 1895.

Here are some wise words to remember Rebecca by: "I early conceived a liking for, and sought every opportunity to relieve the suffering of others."

R is for Rebecca

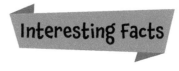

Christiana, Delaware

Christiana is a small hamlet located at the head of the Christina River in Delaware. It was founded in the seventeenth century. Christiana has a colonial history and was home to many of the founding fathers of the United States. George Washington used to stop for rest and a meal in Christiana, because it was along the Kings Road from Philadelphia to Baltimore. The only Revolutionary War battle fought in Delaware was in Christiana, when colonial troops fought off a British invasion at Cooch's Bridge. After the Chesapeake and Delaware canals were constructed during the nineteenth century, the hamlet was bypassed and became less visited. The remains of the hamlet are still there today, with nine historical buildings intact. The hamlet is now an historical district.

Boston, Massachusetts

Boston is the capital of the state of Massachusetts and its most populous city. It is one of the oldest cities in the country and was founded in 1630 by Puritan settlers. Boston is home to many universities and is known as a center of scientific and technical research. Boston was the site of many battles during the Revolutionary War. The first shots of the war were fired on March 5, 1770, when British soldiers fired on a crowd of people who were gathered around a British guard. The first person to die during the Revolutionary War was Crispus Attucks, a mixed-race slave, who died during the Boston Massacre.

Sidney Poitier

Sidney Poitier is an actor, producer, and director. He was born in 1927 in **Miami, Florida**, while his parents were visiting from the Bahamas. Sidney grew up on Cat Island in the **Bahamas**. He returned to the United States when he was a teenager and enlisted in the US Army during World War II, where he served in a medical unit. After his discharge, he auditioned for **the American Negro Theatre** in New York City, but was turned away because of his Bahamian accent. After studying American accents by listening to the radio, he reapplied for the American Negro Theatre six months later and was accepted. He began studying acting and made his Broadway debut in the play *Lysistrata* in 1946.

Sidney acted in many films and plays and was notable for refusing to take roles that required him to play a racial stereotype. In 1958, he became the first Black actor to receive an Academy Award nomination for best actor for his role in *The Defiant Ones*. But he made history with his role in *Lilies of the Field* in 1963, when he won the best actor Oscar award for his role as a handyman who is helping a group of nuns build a chapel. This was the first time a Black actor won a competitive Oscar. Sidney also directed many films. He is a dual citizen of the Bahamas and the United States, and served as

Words You Should Know

» A racial stereotype relies on thinking about the typical qualities thought to be possessed by a group of people. For example, the idea that Black people are lazy or stupid is a racial stereotype.

ambassador to Japan from the Bahamas from 1997 to 2007. In 2009, he was awarded the Presidential Medal of Freedom. In addition to his acting, directing, and producing work, Sidney is an author and has written several books, including memoirs and a suspense novel. He is retired from acting now.

Here are some wise words to remember Sidney by:"History passes the final judgment."

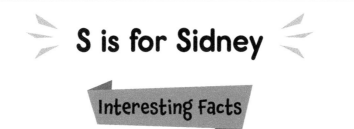

S is for Sidney

Interesting Facts

Miami, Florida

Miami is a city located in southeastern Florida. It was settled in 1825, but was home to the Tequesta for many years before it became a city. Miami is the only city in the United States that was settled by a woman, Julia Tuttle, who was a citrus grower and wealthy woman from Cleveland, Ohio. Black people built much of Miami. In the early twentieth century, 40 percent of the population of Miami was African American or Bahamian. As the city grew in the 1920s, so did the racial tensions in the city. Jim Crow laws kept Black people segregated to a small area of the city, and when landlords began to rent homes to Back people outside of their neighborhood, a gang of white men marched through the streets with torches, telling the Black people to move out or be bombed. Today Miami is known as a tourist destination. It has the busiest cruise port in the world, and many people visit the city over the winter months to escape the cold of winter in the North.

Bahamas

The Commonwealth of the Bahamas is an island nation located in the Caribbean Sea. It is made up of over 700 islands. The capital city is Nassau, located on the island of New Providence. The Bahamas was first settled by the Lucayan, who lived there for many centuries before Columbus arrived there in 1492. The Spanish enslaved the Lucayan natives nearby on the island of Hispaniola and left the Bahamas deserted from about 1513 until 1648 when British colonists settled on the islands. Under British colonial rule, many Europeans settled on the islands and brought enslaved people with them and built plantations. The Bahamas abolished slavery in 1834, and the islands became a destination for escaped slaves from the United States. Today 90 percent of the population of the Bahamas is Black. The Bahamas declared their independence from Great Britain in 1973. Today the islands are a major tourist destination.

The American Negro Theatre

The American Negro Theatre was founded in Harlem, New York, in 1940. It produced nineteen plays before it closed in 1949. The theatre group was founded with four goals: 1) To develop an acting company that was trained in theatrical art and reflected the special talents and culture of Black people. 2) To produce plays that dealt honestly with the lives and concerns of Black people. 3) To maintain connections with other Black theatre groups in the United States. 4) To develop racial pride in theatre. Many famous actors graduated from the American Negro Theatre, including Harry Belafonte, Ruby Dee, Ossie Davis, and Sidney Poitier.

Tarana Burke

Tarana Burke is an activist. She started the #MeToo movement. She was born in the Bronx in New York City in 1973. Tarana's family raised her in a low-income public housing project, where she was attacked, both as a child and as a teenager. This led Tarana to want to make the world a better place. She began working as a teenager with a youth leadership organization called the 21st Century Youth Leadership Movement, where she worked on issues like police brutality, housing inequality, and economic justice. She attended college at Alabama State University. While working in Selma, Alabama, with 21st Century Youth Leadership Movement, Tarana encountered many girls who had been assaulted or molested. In 2005, she created Just Be, Inc., an organization dedicated to ensuring that Black girls had access to safe spaces, support, and other resources.

> ## Words You Should Know
>
> » The #MeToo movement is a social movement that encourages survivors of sexual violence to speak out about their experiences.

In 2017, the #MeToo hashtag went viral, and Tarana emerged as a leading voice in the discussion surrounding sexual assault. In 2018, she founded "Me Too" International, a global nonprofit organization that works with both mainstream and grassroots organizations to address the situations that lead to widespread sexual assault. Tarana has been named the 2017 *Time* magazine person of the year, one of the magazine's 100 most influential people. She was awarded the **2019 Sydney Peace Prize**, and the **Harvard Gleitsman Citizen Activist Award**. She is currently the Senior Director of **Girls for Gender Equity** in Brooklyn, New York. Girls for Gender Equity is an organization that empowers Black girls through various programs and classes.

Here are some wise words to remember Tarana by: "Get up. Stand Up. Speak up. Do something."

T is for Tarana

Interesting Facts

Bronx, New York

The Bronx is one of New York City's boroughs. It was settled in 1639 as part of the New Netherland colony by a Swedish-born man named Jonas Bronck. For many years, the Bronx was home to many groups of immigrant people who arrived in New York City from destinations around the world. In the years from the early 1960s to the early 1980s, the borough experienced several changes. A cross-town expressway was built through the middle of some neighborhoods, which then became slums. High-rise low-income housing projects were also constructed, and many of the white and European residents of the Bronx relocated, leaving a poor Black and Hispanic population in several areas of the Bronx. Since the 1980s, several groups of people have been working to rebuild the neighborhoods that were once poor, and affordable housing is being built.

Selma, Alabama

Selma is a city in the south-central region of Alabama. European explorers first arrived in what would become Selma in about 1732. The city was officially incorporated in 1820. During the Civil War, Selma was important because it was the location of manufacturing of ammunition and Confederate warships. It was the site of the Battle of Selma, which took place in 1865. Selma is well-known for its role during the civil rights movement. It was the starting point for three major marches that took place in the 1960s to ensure equal voting rights and other civil rights. Many sit-ins and protests took place in Selma during the civil rights movement. Today about 80 percent of the population of Selma is Black.

Just Be, Inc.

Just Be, Inc. is a youth organization that focuses on promoting the health and well-being of young women of color. They have several programs that help empower and guide young girls as they grow into their teen years. Just Be, Inc. was founded in 2006.

Sydney Peace Prize

The Sydney Peace Prize is sponsored by the Sydney Peace Foundation, a nonprofit organization linked to the University of Sydney in Australia. The prize promotes justice and nonviolent peacemaking efforts.

Harvard Gleitsman Citizen Activist Award

The Gleitsman Citizen Activist Award is sponsored by Harvard University, and is awarded to a citizen who has sparked positive social change and has encouraged others to do the same. The recipient of the award receives $150,000 and a sculpture designed by Maya Lin, who also designed the Vietnam War Memorial in Washington, DC, and the Civil Rights Memorial in Montgomery, Alabama.

Girls for Gender Equity

Girls for Gender Equity is a nonprofit organization that promotes the well-being of girls, women, and the communities they live in. They have education and physical fitness programs that help girls become strong.

Unita Blackwell

Unita Blackwell was a civil rights activist. She was also the first Black person to be elected mayor of a town in the state of Mississippi. Unita was born in 1933 in **Lula, Mississippi**. Her parents were sharecroppers and the family traveled around the South in search of work. In Mississippi at the time, it was hard for a Black child to receive a quality education because the schools closed down for various planting and harvesting seasons. In 1938, Unita and her mother moved to West Helena, Arkansas, so that Unita could go to school. During the summer months, she still traveled back to Lula to plant and harvest cotton with her grandparents. She had to quit school at the age of fourteen because there was no Black high school where she lived, and she was expected to go to work to raise money to help out her family. After she married, she moved to Mayersville, Mississippi, and became involved in the struggle for civil rights. In June 1964, two activists from the Student Nonviolent Coordinating Committee traveled to Mayersville and spoke at Unita's church about registering to vote. The next week, Unita and a group of seven other people went to the town hall to try to register to vote. A group of white men tried to scare them off, and only two of the people who went were allowed to take the literacy test the town required of registered voters. To make matters worse, the next day, Unita and her husband were fired from their jobs for trying to register to vote.

Words You Should Know

» Civil rights are the rights of an individual to political and social freedom and equality.

But none of that kept Unita from registering to vote. It took her three tries, but she was finally allowed to take the voter registration test and passed!

As an activist in the drive to get voters registered, Unita was often harassed. In 1964, Unita joined the Student Nonviolent Coordinating Committee and organized voter drives across the state of Mississippi. Unita also helped organize a Head Start program for young Black children in Mississippi with the child Development Group of Mississippi. Unita's family filed a lawsuit against the Issaquena Board of Education when their son Jerry and more than 300 Black children were suspended from school for wearing Student Nonviolent Coordinating Committee pins to class. At the time, the school district was still segregated, even though the Supreme Court had ruled that segregation in schools was unconstitutional. The court ruled that the students could not wear the pins, but ordered the school district to integrate. In 1973, Unita began traveling to China, and served for six years as president of the US-China People's Friendship Association. In total, Unita made sixteen diplomatic trips to China. In 1976, Unita was elected mayor of Mayersville, Mississippi. She remained mayor of the town until 2001, making her the first Black female mayor of a town in the state of Mississippi. From 1990 to 1992, she was president of the National Conference of Black Mayors. As part of her work in Mayersville, she worked to find and build affordable housing for the town's residents. In 1992, she was awarded a MacArthur Genius Grant for her work in creating affordable housing in her town and across the state of Mississippi. Unita died in 2019.

Here are some wise words to remember Unita by: "There's no job too big to benefit from a small-town person's perspective, I discovered, just as there's no town too small for thinking big."

U is for Unita

Lula, Mississippi

Lula is a small town located in northwestern Mississippi. The 2010 census reports that the town's population was 298. Seventy-seven percent of the town's residents are Black. It was founded in 1884. Lula has a marker on the Blues Trail, which honors some famous residents who lived there over the years. Lula used to be a much busier town when the railroad still ran through it, and there were a number of juke joints or clubs that operated on weekends, but the railroad has since stopped running through town and the town has gone into decline.

China

The People's Republic of China is the most populous country in the world, with over 1.4 billion people. China was the site of one of the world's first civilizations. Fossils from China show that Peking Man lived there nearly 2.5 million years ago. It is also home to some of the world's oldest writing systems. China has a long, complicated history. Today it is a one-party socialist republic with one of the largest economies on the planet. The Chinese government is often criticized for human rights abuses and the way they treat ethnic minorities.

MacArthur Genius Grant

The MacArthur Fellows Program, also known as the MacArthur Genius Grant, is an award given to between twenty and thirty people each year for "extraordinary originality and dedication in their creative pursuits and a marked capacity for self-direction." Each of the MacArthur Fellows currently receives $625, 000. The award is given by the John D. and Catherine T. MacArthur Foundation. It is awarded with no strings attached. The MacArthur Foundation has been awarding this prize since 1981.

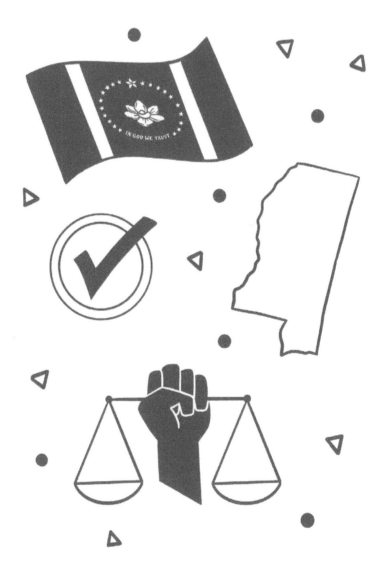

Victor Glover

Victor Glover is an astronaut and pilot. He is a commander in the **US Navy**. He was born in 1976 in Pomona, California. Victor graduated from Ontario High School in Pomona, where he was a quarterback and running back on the school's football team. In 1994, he was awarded Athlete of the Year. He attended California Polytechnic Institute in San Luis Obispo, California, and was awarded a Bachelor of Science degree in in General Engineering in 1999. Victor has earned three master's degrees! He holds a Master of Science degree in Flight Test Engineering from Air University (US Air Force), a Master of Science degree in Systems Engineering from the Naval Postgraduate School, and a Master of Military Operational Art and Science degree from Air University (US Air Force). Victor joined the Navy and completed flight training in 2001. He worked as a test pilot while in the Navy. In 2013, Victor was chosen by NASA to be an astronaut. In August 2018, it was announced that Victor would fly on SpaceX's *Crew Dragon* to the International Space Station, where he would live for six months. This makes

Words You Should Know

» A flight test engineer works with a variety of different kinds of aircraft to make sure they are functioning properly. They test the first models of any new aircraft.

» Systems engineers design and manage complicated systems over their life cycle. The systems can be from a variety of fields, such as software, transportation, product development, or manufacturing.

Victor the first Black astronaut to live on the **International Space Station** for an extended period of time. His mission began in November 2020.

Here are some wise words to remember Victor by: "We want to make sure that we can continue to do new things."

V is for Victor

Interesting Facts

US Navy

The US Navy is the largest navy in the world. It was founded in 1794, but can be traced back further to the Continental Navy, which operated during the US Revolutionary War. Black sailors have been serving in the Navy since before the Civil War. Eight Black sailors earned the Medal of Honor during the Civil War. It also started allowing Black women to serve during World War I. Over 160,000 Black Americans have served in the US Navy since its founding.

International Space Station

The International Space Station is a collaboration between five space agencies who work together to do research in low Earth orbit. The five agencies are from the United States, Russia, Japan, Europe, and Canada. The space station was launched in 1998. It weighs 925,335 pounds! The astronauts aboard the space station also have educational programs for young people, in addition to the scientific research they do. On the space station, they cover the windows when the astronauts are sleeping because you can see sixteen sunrises and sunsets from aboard the space station per day.

Wally Amos

Wally Amos is a television personality, entrepreneur, and author. He was born in Tallahassee, Florida, in 1936. Wally was raised in Tallahassee until he was twelve years old, when he moved to New York City to live with his aunt. While in New York, he enrolled at the Food Trades Vocational School. Wally loved to cook from an early age. He dropped out of high school to join the Air Force and earned his high school equivalency degree while in the military. Wally served in the Air Force for three years. After the Air Force, Wally returned to New York City and went to college to study to become a secretary. His first job after graduation was at the William Morris Agency, a talent agency that represents celebrities. There, he signed Simon & Garfunkel and represented musicians like Sam Cooke, Diana Ross and the Supremes, and Marvin Gaye. Wally's Aunt Della had a special chocolate chip cookie recipe that Wally adapted, and he would send cookies to people he was hoping to sign. In 1975, a friend of his suggested that he open a store to sell his cookies. That year, he opened the first Famous Amos cookie store. Soon, Famous Amos cookies could be found in grocery stores throughout the United States! In addition to selling cookies and representing celebrities, Wally works to make sure adults and children learn to read. He hosted a television show called *Learn to Read* and has worked closely with the Literacy Volunteers of America. He has helped thousands of people learn to read.

Here are some wise words to remember Victor by: "Life is just a mirror, and what you see out there, you must first see inside of you."

W is for Wally

Interesting Facts

Tallahassee, Florida

Tallahassee is a city in northern Florida. It is the state capital. The city was founded in 1824. Tallahassee is located in what was known as the Cotton Belt of Florida, which relied heavily on slave labor to run its plantations. During the Civil War, Tallahassee was the only Confederate state capital east of the Mississippi River that was not attacked by Union forces. In 1887, the Normal College for Colored Students was founded in Tallahassee to teach Black students. At the time, colleges in Florida were segregated, and there was a need for a school to teach Black students in the state. Today the school is Florida A&M University. According to the 2010 US census, Tallahassee has a 35 percent Black population.

The Supremes

The Supremes were an all-female singing group from Detroit, Michigan, that performed during the 1960s. They recorded for Motown Records. Out of all the groups that Motown Records produced, the Supremes were the most successful, with twelve number-one hit singles on the Billboard Hot 100. They were also the most commercially successful of any American singing group. They helped pave the way for other Black singers and musicians to build successful careers.

Marvin Gaye

Marvin Gaye was a singer, songwriter, and producer. He also recorded for Motown Records and helped shape the sound of

Motown. He had a string of popular hits during the time he recorded, but is well known for his protest anthem, "What's Going On," which he wrote after witnessing an incident of police brutality. Marvin Gaye was inducted into the Rock and Roll Hall of Fame in 1987. He died in 1984.

Famous Amos
Famous Amos is a brand of cookies that was founded by Wally Amos in Los Angeles, California. Wally opened his first cookie store in 1975 and sold $300,000 worth of cookies his first year. The next year, he sold over $1 million in cookies! The store was so successful that Wally reached out to other retailers and began selling his cookies in supermarkets.

Literacy Volunteers of America
Literacy Volunteers of America was founded in 1962 by Ruth Johnson Colvin, who designed a way to tutor adults to learn to read. In 2002, the Literacy Volunteers of America merged with another organization, Laubach Literacy International. They now operate ProLiteracy, an international organization that helps teach adults to read and write. The organization is based in Syracuse, New York, and operates in thirty-five countries.

Xernona Clayton

Xernona Clayton is a civil rights leader and broadcasting executive. She was born in 1930 in Muskogee, Oklahoma. Her parents helped manage Indian affairs in Muskogee and worked with disadvantaged Native Americans. After she graduated from high school, Xernona attended Tennessee State University and graduated in 1952. After college, she moved to Chicago and worked as an undercover agent for the Urban League. Her job was to try to prove that Black people were being discriminated against when they applied for jobs. She attended the University of Chicago and taught in public elementary and high schools. In Chicago, Xernona met her first husband Ed Clayton, who was the executive editor of *Jet magazine*. They moved to Los Angeles in 1960. While in Los Angeles, Xernona was active in political campaigns, and when John F. Kennedy gave a speech asking people to work with those less fortunate, Xernona volunteered to help organize a group to work with about one hundred high school dropouts. About eighty of them went back to school and earned their diplomas.

In 1965, Dr. Martin Luther King Jr. asked the Claytons to move to Atlanta, and they did, but Xernona's husband died suddenly the next year. In Atlanta, Xernona didn't let the death of her husband stop her from making a difference. She helped integrate hospitals as part of the Doctors Committee on Implementation of Civil Rights. When she saw that there were few Black presenters on television, Xernona pointed it out and was hired by WAGA-TV as the host of *Themes and Variations*, which later became the *Xernona Clayton Show*. The program made her the first Black on-air television personality in the South during the years it aired, 1968–1975. After Turner Broadcasting was started in 1979, Xernona went to work for them in a career that lasted more than thirty years. When she retired from Turner Broadcasting, she was Vice President for Urban Affairs. Xernona continues to live in Atlanta, where she is still active in civil rights and civic affairs.

Here are some wise words to remember Xernona by: "We're not where we want to be. It might not change tonight. It might not change tomorrow. Tomorrow may be another day. We're going to keep inspiring. We're going to keep educating. We've got to keep fueling the fire with the burning desire to do better."

X is for Xernona

Interesting Facts

Muskogee, Oklahoma

Muskogee is a city in Oklahoma. In 1806, French fur traders set up a temporary village in what is now Muskogee, but the city was first settled in 1817. It is named for the Muscogee Creek, a tribe of Native Americans from the southeast United States who were forced off their land and sent to Oklahoma with their slaves after the Indian Removal Act was passed in 1830.

Urban League

The National Urban League was founded in 1910. It is a civil rights organization that tries to empower Black Americans and other underserved groups, and to ensure equality and social justice. The Urban League is headquartered in New York City and works with local leaders in thirty-seven states and the District of Columbia to ensure the civil rights of Black people are upheld.

Jet Magazine

Jet is a weekly American magazine that reports on issues of importance to the Black community in news, culture, and entertainment. It was first published in 1951 and reported on the civil rights movement. It is no longer in print, but can be found in digital format online. *Jet's* sister magazine is *Ebony,* which also focuses on news of importance to the Black community.

Themes and Variations

Themes and Variations was a television show hosted by Xernona Clayton. The show later became *The Xernona Clayton Show*. Xernona named the show after a column she wrote for the *Atlanta Voice*. It made her the first Black on-air personality in the South. In the show's debut, Xernona convinced the Grand Dragon of the Ku Klux Klan to leave the organization. The show was on the air from 1968 to 1975.

Turner Broadcasting

Turner Broadcasting is a television and media company that is headquartered in Atlanta, Georgia. The stations TBS, TNT, CNN, and TruTV are all properties of Turner Broadcasting. The company began as a billboard company in Savannah, Georgia, that was owned by Robert Edward Turner. When he passed away, his son Ted inherited the company and expanded it into television and radio. Turner Broadcasting merged with Time Warner in 1996.

Yolanda King

Yolanda King was a civil rights activist and the first-born child of **Dr. Martin Luther King Jr.** and his wife Coretta Scott King. She was born in 1955 in **Montgomery, Alabama**. Growing up in Montgomery during the civil rights struggle, Yolanda was able to witness history being made first-hand. In 1956, her home was bombed by a group of white supremacists. Yolanda and her mother were not injured during the explosion. In the fall of 1965, Yolanda enrolled at Spring Street Elementary School. She wrote her first play when she was eight years old, and began speaking publicly at the age of ten, sometimes filling in for her parents. After writing her play, Yolanda enrolled in the only integrated drama school at the time in her area. When she was twelve years old, her father was assassinated. Yolanda flew to Memphis, where Dr. King had been shot, and marched with the sanitation workers her father had been in Memphis to help organize. Yolanda was president of her sophomore and junior classes at Grady High School.

After high school, Yolanda went to Smith College in Boston, Massachusetts. After graduating from Smith, she went to work for the Martin Luther King Jr. Center for Nonviolent Social Change, and was founding director of the King Center's Cultural Affairs Program. Yolanda became an activist and an actress. She worked for **Habitat for Humanity**, she was a

Words You Should Know

» A white supremacist is someone who believes that the white race is superior to all other races and should determine how society operates.

member of the Southern Christian Leadership Conference, she sponsored the **Women's International League for Peace and Freedom,** she worked for the Human Rights Campaign, and she had a lifelong membership in the NAACP. She went back to school and earned a master's degree in theatre from New York University. She starred as **Rosa Parks** in the TV miniseries *King,* which aired in 1978. She was the founder and head of Higher Ground Productions, whose mission was to promote "inner peace, unity, and global transformation." Yolanda died in 2007.

Here are some wise words to remember Yolanda by: "What we need to do is learn to respect and embrace our differences until our differences don't make a difference in how we are treated."

Y is for Yolanda

Interesting Facts

Dr. Martin Luther King Jr.

The Reverend Dr. Martin Luther King Jr. was a minister and the most well-known civil rights activist of the 1950s and 1960s. He was born in 1929 in Atlanta, Georgia, and was the son of a minister and civil rights activist. Dr. King embraced a philosophy of peaceful, nonviolent resistance, and led marches and participated in protests for Black people's right to vote, for desegregation, labor rights, and other basic human rights, like equality. He was the first president of the Southern Christian Leadership Conference, a very active civil rights organization. In 1964, Dr. King won the Nobel Peace Prize for his efforts to ensure Black equality. He was a gifted speaker, and thousands of people would gather to listen to his speeches, many of which are still replayed today. He was assassinated in Memphis, Tennessee, on April 4, 1968, while organizing a garbage workers' strike.

Montgomery, Alabama

Montgomery is the capital city of the state of Alabama. It was incorporated in 1819 after two towns merged to form the city. The city is situated along the Alabama River and, prior to the Civil War, it was used to transport slaves. Montgomery grew quickly before the Civil War because it grew rich from the cotton that the slaves farmed for plantation owners. It was home to one of the largest slave markets in the South. During the Civil War, Montgomery was captured by Union forces in 1865 at the Battle of Montgomery. It was the first city in the United States to install citywide electric streetcars. After World War II, the Black soldiers who returned to Montgomery were dissatisfied with life under Jim Crow laws and began to organize and discuss their civil rights more vocally. Montgomery was an important city during the civil rights movement. It was the destination for three marches that were held between Selma, Alabama, and Montgomery. According to the 2010 Census, the city is 56.6 percent Black.

Habitat for Humanity
Habitat for Humanity is a nonprofit organization that seeks to help families build and improve the places they live in. It was founded in 1976 in Americus, Georgia, by Millard and Linda Fuller. Habitat for Humanity builds new homes and repairs existing homes for low-income families across the United States.

Women's International League for Peace and Freedom
The Women's International League for Peace and Freedom is a nonprofit organization that seeks to promote peace and end war by empowering women. It was founded in the Netherlands in 1915, during World War I, when a group of 1,136 women from both warring and neutral nations gathered to discuss how to end the war and make peace. The group sees a direct link between women's rights and the struggle for peace. They believe that women should have an equal say in peacemaking efforts, and that more women should be in positions of authority to make lasting changes.

Rosa Parks

Rosa Parks was a civil rights activist from Montgomery, Alabama. She is best known for her role in sparking the Montgomery bus boycott. In 1955, she was on a bus in Montgomery and was ordered by the bus driver to give up her seat to a white passenger. Rosa refused to vacate her seat and was arrested. She was not the first person in Montgomery to refuse to give up her seat, but it was thought that she was the best person to go through the courts to challenge segregation on the buses. She inspired a boycott of Montgomery buses that lasted a full year. In later years, Rosa Parks became active in the Black Power movement. She died in 2005.

Zoe Saldana

Zoe Saldana is an actress. She was born in 1978 in Passaic, New Jersey. Her family is bilingual and they speak both Spanish and English. When she was nine years old, her father died, and her mother took her and her two sisters to the Dominican Republic. Zoe discovered a love of dance while living in the Dominican Republic and studied ballet. Her family returned to the United States when she was seventeen. She began performing with the Faces theatre group in New York City. The plays the theatre group performed were written to provide positive messages to young people about topics such as substance abuse and sexuality. Her film career began with the movie *Center Stage*, about a ballet dancer. She has gone on to become the second-highest-grossing actress of all time due to her roles in three of the highest-earning movies of all time (*Avatar, Avengers: Infinity War,* and *Avengers: Endgame*). She is a supporter of FINCA International, a micro-finance corporation, and founded BESE, a digital media company that seeks to "combat the lack of diversity in the mainstream media."

Here are some wise words to remember Zoe by: "Happiness is nothing but temporary moments here and there—and I love those. But I would be bored out of my mind if I were happy all the time."

Z is for Zoe

Interesting Facts

Passaic, New Jersey

Passaic is a city in the state of New Jersey. It is located north of Newark on the Passaic River. The city was first settled by Dutch traders in 1678. As the city grew, it became a center for textile mills. In 1926, thirty-six thousand textile workers walked off their jobs during the Passaic Textile Strike. They were protesting cuts to their wages. They won the right to have their wages stay the same. Passaic is known as "the birthplace of television" after an experimental television station began transmitting from Passaic in 1931. It was the first television station to transmit a signal into people's homes, and the first television station to broadcast a movie.

Dominican Republic

The Dominican Republic is a Caribbean nation that shares the island of Hispaniola with Haiti. It was home to the Taino people until Columbus arrived in 1492. Within a few years of the Spaniards' arrival, many of the Taino had died off due to smallpox and other diseases. Columbus landed in what is now the Dominican Republic on his first voyage to the New World in 1492, and he claimed the island of Hispaniola for Spain. In 1501, the Spanish began importing slaves from Africa. Sugar cane soon became a major crop on the island, and slave labor was needed to work the sugar plantations. In 1821, the country declared its independence from Spain as Spanish Haiti. Under Spanish Haitian rule, the island outlawed slavery. In 1843, the Dominican Republic side of the island revolted against the

Haitian government and won their independence. Today, the Dominican Republic is the Caribbean nation most visited by tourists and is known for its golf courses and beaches.

FINCA International
FINCA International is a nonprofit organization that provides microfinance loans to people in developing nations. It was founded in 1985 by John Hatch. It operates in twenty countries.

BESE
BESE is the digital media company that was founded by Zoe Saldana. Its mission is to "reshape the cultural narrative by shining light on the untold stories that reflect today's America." BESE can be found at www.bese.com. They particularly highlight stories about Latinx culture and the Latinx community.

About the Author

B orn in Port-au-Prince, **M.J. Fievre, B.S. Ed**, is a longtime educator whose publishing career began as a teenager in her native Haiti. She is the author of the middle-grade book series, Young Trailblazers, and the picture book series, *A Cat Named Sam*. M.J. earned a bachelor's degree in education from Barry University. A seasoned K–12 teacher, a creator of safe spaces, and an initiator of difficult conversations, she spent much time building up her students, helping them feel comfortable in their own skin, and affirming their identities. Her close relationships with parents and students led her to look more closely at how we can balance protecting a child's innocence with preparing them for the realities of life. She has taught creative writing workshops to children at the O Miami Poetry Festival and the Miami Art Museum, as well as in various schools in Santa Cruz de la Sierra (Bolivia), Port-au-Prince (Haiti), and South Florida. She's also been a keynote speaker at various universities, colleges, and libraries, and has served as a panelist at the Association of Writers & Writing Programs Conference (AWP). M.J. is available for book club meetings, podcast presentations, interviews and other author events.

About the Illustrator

K **im Balacuit** is an illustrator and designer currently living in sunny Florida. Her background in graphic design, animation, and illustration have allowed her to work in both children's media and picture books. When she's not buried in artwork, you can find her reading at the beach, practicing (and failing) at roller skating, daydreaming about dogs, or finding the spiciest foods to eat. You can visit her work at www. kimbalacuit.com.

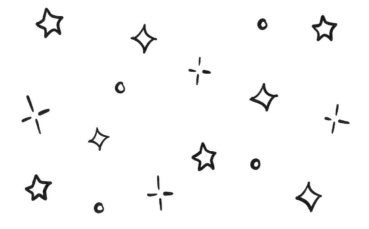

By the Same Author
Children's Books

Young Trailblazers: The
Book of Black Inventors
and Scientists

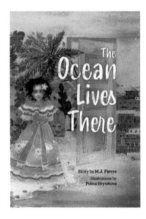

The Ocean Lives There

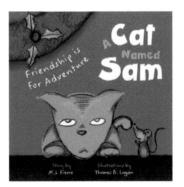

A Cat Named Sam:
Friendship is for Adventure

By the Same Author
Young Adult Books

*Badass Black Girl:
Quotes, Questions, and
Affirmations for Teens*

*Empowered Black Girl:
Joyful Affirmations and
Words of Resilience*

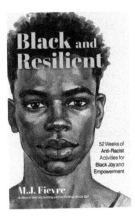

*Black and Resilient:
52 Weeks of Anti-Racist
Activities for Black Joy and
Empowerment*

*Resilient Black Girl:
52 Weeks of Anti-Racist
Activities for Black Joy and
Resilience*

DragonFruit, an imprint of Mango Publishing, publishes high-quality children's books to inspire a love of lifelong learning in readers. DragonFruit publishes a variety of titles for kids, including children's picture books, nonfiction series, toddler activity books, pre-K activity books, science and education titles, and ABC books. Beautiful and engaging, our books celebrate diversity, spark curiosity, and capture the imaginations of parents and children alike.

Mango Publishing, established in 2014, publishes an eclectic list of books by diverse authors. We were named the Fastest Growing Independent Publisher by Publishers Weekly in 2019 and 2020. Our success is bolstered by our main goal, which is to publish high-quality books that will make a positive impact in people's lives.

Our readers are our most important resource; we value your input, suggestions, and ideas. We'd love to hear from you—after all, we are publishing books for you!

Please stay in touch with us and follow us at:
Instagram: @dragonfruitkids
Facebook: Mango Publishing
Twitter: @MangoPublishing
LinkedIn: Mango Publishing
Pinterest: Mango Publishing

Sign up for our newsletter at www.mangopublishinggroup.com and receive a free book! Join us on Mango's journey to change publishing, one book at a time.

CPSIA information can be obtained
at www.ICGtesting.com
Printed in the USA
JSHW041515290722
28702JS00005B/11

9 781642 507829